Vaṅgīsa

An Early Buddhist Poet

Pali text edited and translated by

John D. Ireland

Buddhist Publication Society
Kandy • Sri Lanka

Published in 1997

Buddhist Publication Society
P.O. Box 61
54, Sangharaja Mawatha
Kandy, Sri Lanka

ISBN 955–24–0161–5

Typeset at the BPS

Printed in Sri Lanka by
Karunaratne & Sons Ltd.
Colombo 10

THE WHEEL PUBLICATION NO. 417/418

Contents

Introduction 1

Vaṅgīsa's Verses 11

I. Departed (*Nikkhantaṃ*) 11
II. Disliking (*Aratiṃ*) 12
III. Despising the Well-behaved (*Pesalā-atimaññanā*) 13
IV. Ānanda 14
V. Well-spoken (*Subhāsitā*) 16
VI. Sāriputta 17
VII. The Invitation Ceremony (*Pavāraṇā*) 17
VIII. More than a Thousand (*Parosahassaṃ*) 18
IX. Overcoming (*Abhibhuyya*) 19
X. Koṇḍañña 20
XI. Moggallāna 21
XII. Gaggarā 22
XIII. Vaṅgīsa (1) 22
XIV. Vaṅgīsa (2) 24
XV. Nigrodhakappa 25

Appendices 31

Notes to the Pāli Text 38

Notes to the Translation 40

Introduction

The *Theragāthā*, the Verses of the Elders, is a work found in the Khuddaka Nikāya of the Sutta Piṭaka of the Pāli Canon. As its name indicates, this is a collection of verses ascribed to various elder monks, mostly celebrating their attainment of arahantship. As with a number of other works in the Pāli Canon, such as the Aṅguttara Nikāya and the Itivuttaka, the Theragāthā is divided into sections (*nipāta*) with progressively increasing numbers of verses. It begins with a section of single verses, then continues with pairs, triplets, and so forth. In the later sections this system breaks down and the number of verses which the poems actually contain only approximate to the number of the section.

The present work is a translation accompanying the original Pāli text of the final and longest section of the Theragāthā, the *Mahānipāta* or "Great Section." This is a self-contained anthology of fourteen poems with seventy-one verses, composed by a single elder, the Venerable Vaṅgīsa. Although not indicated in the text, the various occasions for the composition and recitation of these poems is to be found in the commentary. These in turn are a summary of the information supplied by the Vaṅgīsa-saṃyutta of the Saṃyutta Nikāya, where we find a parallel version of these poems embedded in a series of short suttas giving the circumstances of their composition. Interestingly, the two versions of the poems are not identical, though the differences are mostly slight. They consist mainly of dialectical variants from a time when Pāli was an oral literature being collected from the several dialects of Māgadhī, the actual spoken language of that region of Northern India in which the Buddha and his early followers lived and preached the Dhamma.

The author of these poems, the Venerable Vaṅgīsa, was designated by the Buddha as the foremost of his disciples with respect to spontaneity of speech (*paṭibhānavantānaṃ*, A I 24). This gift is evidently a reference to the Parosahassa Sutta (S I 192–93) where, after reciting a poem (No. VIII of the translation), the Buddha asked Vaṅgīsa whether it had been devised by him beforehand or had occurred to him "on the spot" (*thānaso va taṃ paṭibhanti*). When Vaṅgīsa affirmed the latter, the Buddha invited him to compose some more verses, and the result was the next poem (No. IX).

Apart from what we can glean from the poems themselves and the suttas of the Vaṅgīsa-saṃyutta, we know very little about the Venerable Vaṅgīsa himself. The commentary (ThagA III 180–81) says he was a brahmin by birth and that, prior to meeting the Buddha, he made a living by tapping the skulls of deceased people and telling thereby where the owners had been reborn. The Buddha tested him by presenting him with several skulls, including that of an arahant. He was successful with his first few guesses, but when he came to the arahant's skull he was mystified, for an arahant is not reborn anywhere. He decided to enter the Order to discover the secret. He was ordained by the Elder Nigrodhakappa and later became an arahant. The commentary adds that after composing some verses in praise of the Buddha he gained a reputation as a poet.

According to the Apadāna (Ap II 497) Vaṅgīsa was so called both because he was born in the country of Vaṅga (modern Bengal) and also because he was a "master (*īsa*) of the spoken word (*vacana*)." In Buddhist Sanskrit works, such as the *Mahāvastu*, his name appears unambiguously as Vāgīśa, "Lord of Speech." This is, of course, an assumed name and we do not know his actual personal name, as is common with individuals in this early Buddhist literature. "Lord of Speech," or perhaps better, "Master of Words," is an apt title for a poet.

The poems themselves give us the picture of a man of sensitive and artistic temperament who found it difficult to control his innate sensuality, manifest in his attachment to the opposite sex. He would have appreciated this passage from the Aṅguttara Nikāya: "They fetter him who has forgotten mindfulness, with gaze and smile, disordered dress, sweet blandishments ..." (A III 69). Furthermore, he was proud of his gift of poetic invention, but recognized this pride as a fault to be overcome (No. III). The sole reference in the poems to his life before he met the Buddha says only that he was obsessed by the poetic art (No. XIII). All of this tends to cast doubt on the authenticity of the bizarre tale of the skull-tapping brahmin. In the absence of any evidence to the contrary it is perhaps best to be noted as a curiosity. The importance of Vaṅgīsa lies in his talent as a poet, a gift that must have been nurtured and developed over a period of time before the present poems were composed. We might also conclude that for someone able to compose verse spontaneously, as Vaṅgīsa could, his output might well have been enormous. The few "religious" poems that have survived may be only a small fraction of an opus that is now lost forever.

After these preliminary remarks I ought to discuss some points arising from the poems themselves, but first I wish to make a general observation concerning the translation. My aim has been to convey the exact verbal meaning of the poems, and for this purpose I felt a literal prose translation would be more suitable than one in verse. Moreover, a verse translation could be positively misleading if it made a pretense of conveying the "feel" of the original poems; hence also the decision to reproduce the Pāli text alongside the translation. In recent decades much scholarly work has been done in restoring and correcting the text of the Theragāthā and I took the opportunity to incorporate the results of such research into this edited version of Vaṅgīsa's verses. I leave the assessment of Vaṅgīsa as a poet to those better qualified to judge. Pāli metre and Indian poetics in general are difficult subjects of which the present translator has little knowledge.

My aim in both the text and the translation has been to adhere as closely as possible to what was originally intended by the poet and to the meaning understood by his contemporaries. With this in view the translation occasionally departs from the interpretations of particular words and phrases proposed by the (later) commentaries. For instance, in v.1221 we find the term *maggajina.* The commentary interprets this as "a path-victor" or "conqueror (by means) of the path." In the Cunda Sutta (Sn 83–90) *maggajina* is the first of the four kinds of *samaṇa* (ascetic) listed there. According to the commentary, "One who has overcome all defilements by means of the path is called a path-victor" (SnA I 162). However, as K.R. Norman has pointed out, the suffix *-jina* is unlikely to mean "conqueror" here, but was a dialect form from Skt. *jñā* (to know). Hence it is probable that the commentary is mistaken and that the word originally meant "a path-knower." I have translated it in this way on the assumption that this was what Vaṅgīsa himself intended by the expression.

Another innovation is my translation of the term *puthujjana* as "outsiders" (vv. 1217, 1271). This term is usually translated "ordinary persons," "worldlings," "manyfolk," etc., taking *puthu* in its sense of "numerous," "various" (= Vedic *pṛthu*). However, another meaning of *puthu* is "separate," "apart" (= Vedic *pṛthak*). Although this sense was deemed inappropriate for *puthujjana* by earlier translators and the PTS Dictionary, there is no real reason why it could not be so understood. The term refers to those people who are apart from, separate from, those in possession of the Dhamma of the noble ones (*ariya*), the Buddha and his disciples. The commentaries use *puthujjana* to refer to anyone and everyone who has not yet reached at least the path of stream-entry; thereafter they become noble disciples (*ariya-sāvakā*) and lose their designation as *puthujjana.* It is possible, however, that the term was originally used in a still more restricted sense, as referring to those incapable (*abhabbo*) of understanding the Dhamma, in contrast to the *viññū* (wise, intelligent persons) who could do so when it was taught to them. Being apart from Dhamma, the *puthujjana* are established in what is not-Dhamma (*adhamma* or unrighteousness). They are unable to relate to the Buddha's Teaching because they are attached to and blinded by the many wrong and speculative views that are at variance with the Dhamma.

I decided to use "Fortunate One" as a translation of *bhagavā* (*bhagavantu*). This seems to be closer to what was intended than the common rendering "Blessed One," which could give rise to the query, "Blessed by whom?" Again, "Lord" or even "Exalted One" is suggestive of dominance over others by a god-like being, which is surely not intended here. All such renderings have strong theistic overtones and so can be misleading. In Hinduism Bhagavān is used as a term for God, and thus in that context "Lord," e.g. "Lord Krishna," is appropriate.

In translating Vaṅgīsa's verses my guiding principle has been to leave as few words as possible untranslated. With this aim "monk" is used for *bhikkhu* and "god" for *deva*, words which I had left in the original Pāli in an earlier translated work. I decided to retain Dhamma and Tathāgata, which are generally held to elude satisfactory rendering into English. But the occurrence of the word*nāga* in v.1240 became an exception to the rule. One meaning of*nāga* is "bull elephant." *Nāga* is used as an epithet of the Buddha and his arahant disciples (see also v.1279), and I had first thought to translate v.1240 thus: "You are called an elephant, Fortunate One…" However, in English, instead of suggesting the intended feelings of reverence and awe, on initial encounter this might well be taken in a pejorative sense (of ungainliness, clumsiness); hence I decided to leave it untranslated. In Thag 691–704 various attributes of the Buddha are equated with parts of the elephant—feet, tusks, trunk, and so forth. The word *nāga* is also used for the serpent (cobra) and a class of semi-divine beings, depicted in art as half-human and half-snake; perhaps it originally referred to certain indigenous tribal peoples who worshipped the cobra. A*nāga* cult still exists in India today.

The subject matter of the poems is diverse. The first four poems show Vaṅgīsa articulating his inner struggle to overcome various failings and elementary obstacles: sensual thoughts, doubt, attachment, views, pride and conceit, ways of thinking not to be entertained by one who has gone forth into homelessness. Foremost among these failings is sensual desire, which arises through unguarded contact with desirable sights, sounds, etc. In the first poem these objects of desire are conceived as devices of Māra, the Evil One, to overpower the mind and prevent progress upon the path. The fourth poem shows how arisen sensual desires can be extinguished and dispelled by appropriate attitudes and meditation practices. In this latter poem it may be questioned whether it is actually the Venerable Ānanda who is here addressed as "Gotama" or the Buddha himself. However, there is no problem if we understand that Vaṅgīsa's query *is* being answered by the Buddha, whose word was memorized and transmitted through his disciple Ānanda.

The fifth poem is unique in being a verse summary of a sermon by the Buddha on truth as the "well-spoken word." This poem is also to be found in the Suttanipāta (Sn 451–54), and the fact that the three versions hardly differ may indicate that it enjoyed wide popularity. The sixth is the first of three sketches of the Buddha's disciples. Here it is Sāriputta; the others are Koṇḍañña (No. X) and Mahāmoggallāna (No. XI). This poem gives a rare glimpse of Sāriputta as a skilled teacher and speaker able to captivate the monks with his pleasant voice.

"All are the Fortunate One's sons ..." (v.1237): that the Buddha's arahant disciples are regarded as his "sons" is a recurrent idea in the Theragāthā and elsewhere. In the Itivuttaka the Buddha says: "Monks, ... you are my own legitimate sons, born from my mouth, born of Dhamma, fashioned by Dhamma, heirs of Dhamma, not heirs of material things" (It 100). In v.1248 Vaṅgīsa calls the Elder Koṇḍañña "the Awakened One's heir" and Nigrodhakappa in v.1279 "a true son of the *nāga*" (i.e. of the Buddha). The idea is extended in Thag 536, where Kāludāyin actually addresses Suddhodana, the Buddha's natural father, as his grandfather! It is the tradition that the Buddha had a son named Rāhula who became a monk. But the Venerable Rāhula found in the Sutta Piṭaka, when called the

Buddha's son, has no special claim to that position over and above that of any other disciple. In the suttas Rāhula is portrayed as the ideal novice monk, eager for instruction in the Teaching.

Poems VIII and IX extol the Buddha and his Teaching and in v.1241 the poet actually refers to himself by name. No. XII consists of just a single verse praising the Buddha. No. XIII is Vaṅgīsa's declaration of *aññā*, the attainment of final knowledge or arahantship. Up to this point the differences between the versions of the poems in the Theragāthā and the Vaṅgīsa-saṃyutta have been quite minor. But the verses of this poem are so different from those of the Vaṅgīsa Sutta in the Saṃyutta Nikāya that it should be regarded as a separate poem. It is therefore inserted here as Poem XIV for the sake of completeness and for purposes of comparison. Although the subject matter of both poems is the same, the Saṃyutta version is half the length of the other, with only five stanzas, in contrast to the ten of the Theragāthā version. Circumstantial evidence suggests the shorter poem was the original, which was later expanded, either by Vaṅgīsa himself or someone else, to create the longer poem.

The Vaṅgīsa Sutta concludes the Saṃyutta collection and is in keeping with what has gone before, in as much as none of the poems exceed five stanzas in length. Also the Vaṅgīsa-saṃyutta is found in the first and probably the most ancient division of the Saṃyutta Nikāya, the Sagāthāvagga. In contrast, the longer poem comes almost at the end of the Theragāthā and is followed by yet one more, the final and inordinately long Nigrodhakappa poem of seventeen stanzas, which concludes this entire collection. It is known that the Theragāthā grew over a long period of time and received additional material even up to the time of Emperor Asoka. It is therefore more than likely that these final two poems came into existence after the Saṃyutta anthology was finalized.

How the longer poem was constructed from the shorter is best seen by analyzing each of the Pāli *gāthā* (stanzas) into their constituent four *pāda* (metrical units). Thus the first three stanzas of the shorter poem were expanded to five by the insertion of extra *pāda*. All the original *pāda* were retained, but not in the same order. Stanzas six and seven of the longer poem, referring to the Four Noble Truths, have nothing corresponding to them in the shorter poem and are therefore new material. Three *pāda* from the last two stanzas of the shorter poem were discarded (fourth stanza, *pāda* 3; fifth stanza, *pāda* 1 and 2), but the rest utilized to make the final three stanzas of the longer poem.

The final poem in this anthology (No. XV), as already indicated, is missing from the Saṃyutta collection. However, a corresponding version is found at Sn 343–58, called there variously the Vaṅgīsa Sutta, Kappa Sutta, or Nigrodhakappa Sutta. Apart from its much greater length, this poem differs from the preceding poems in a number of other ways. The fact that it directly addresses the Buddha and is in a more ornate, even extravagant style sets it apart from the simpler, unvarnished verse of the earlier poems. Expressions such as that in v.1266 referring to "the thousand-eyed Sakka," are characteristic of a late period of Pāli composition. And indeed, the comparison of the Buddha's voice to the honking of a goose (v.1270) is a device suggestive of the highly ornate poetry of a much later age. That the elder is variously called Nigrodhakappa, Kappa, Kappiya, Kappāyana, is, of course, to conform to the requirements of the metre.

Although the Nigrodhakappa poem is ostensibly a request to the Buddha for information about the attainment of the deceased elder, Vaṅgīsa's teacher, the manner and persistence of the "urge to speak Dhamma" and other such expressions point to a deeper meaning. An underlying idea is that the Buddha alone, when proclaiming the Dhamma, is capable of producing a profound effect upon his hearers (the literal meaning of *sāvaka*). He is able to establish them on the noble path of the *sotāpanna*, etc., at least those who are ready to receive it, by the Dhamma-words issuing forth through his speech and apparently without any prior practice on the part of the recipients. This is a special gift exercised by the

Buddha alone and not by his disciples. Although this idea is not taken up to any extent by the Theravāda, which stresses the human side of the Buddha, it was a factor affecting other Indian schools of Buddhism and the so-called Mahāyāna, which tended to emphasize the Buddha's transcendental nature.

Both the Theragāthā and the first volume of the Saṃyutta Nikāya, where these verses are found, were first translated by Mrs. Rhys Davids under the respective titles *Psalms of the Brethren* (PTS 1913) and *Kindred Sayings I* (PTS 1917). The Theragāthā was retranslated more recently by K.R. Norman as *Elders' Verses I* (PTS 1969). The present translator has relied heavily upon Norman's erudite translation and his copious notes to the original Pāli text.

Vaṅgīsa's Verses

I. Departed
(*Nikkhantaṃ*)

As a new monk, recently gone forth, lustful passion was aroused in the Venerable Vangisa when he saw a number of women adorned in all their finery who had come to visit the monastery. He dispelled this lust, recording the experience in these verses:

1209. nikkhantaṃ vata maṃ santaṃ agārasmānagāriyaṃ
vitakkā upadhāvanti pagabbhā kaṇhato ime.

1209. Alas! Now that I have departed from home to the homeless state, these reckless thoughts from the Dark One[1] come upon me.

1210. uggaputtā mahissāsā sikkhitā daḷhadhammino
samantā parikireyyuṃ sahassaṃ apalāyinaṃ.

1210. Mighty warriors, great archers, trained, steady bowmen, one thousand fearless men, might surround me on all sides.

1211. sace pi ettakā bhiyyo āgamissanti itthiyo
n'eva maṃ byādhayissanti dhamme svamhi patiṭṭhito.

1211. Even if more women than these will come,[2] they will not cause me to waver, for I am firmly established in the teaching.

1212. sakkhiṃ hi me sutaṃ etaṃ buddhassādiccabandhuno
nibbānagamanaṃ maggaṃ tattha me nirato mano.

1212. In his presence I heard from the Awakened One, the Kinsman of the Sun, of this path leading to nibbāna; it is there that my mind is attached.

1213. evañ ce maṃ viharantaṃ pāpima upagacchasi
tathā maccu karissāmi na me maggaṃ udikkhasi.

1213. Evil One, while I am living thus, if you assail me, so shall I act, O Death, that you will not see my path.

II. Disliking
(*Aratiṃ*)

While staying at Alavi the Venerable Vangisa's teacher, the Elder Nigrodhakappa, after returning from the alms round, remained in seclusion for long periods. On one occasion, when discontent arose in the mind of the Venerable Vangisa and his mind was tormented by lust, he composed these verses to reprove himself and to dispel the conflicting emotions that harassed him:

1214. aratiṃ ratiñ ca pahāya sabbaso gehasitañ ca vitakkaṃ
vanathaṃ na kareyya kuhiñci nibbanathāvanatho
sa hi bhikkhu.

1214. Entirely giving up disliking and liking, and the thinking associated with the life of a householder, one should not have craving for anything. He indeed is a monk who is wholly without craving.

1215. yam idha pathaviñ ca vehāsaṃ rūpagataṃ jagatogadhaṃ
kiñci
parijiyyati sabbam aniccaṃ evaṃ samecca caranti
mutattā.

1215. Whatever there is here of form, inhabiting the earth and the sky, immersed in the world,[3] all is impermanent and decaying. So understanding, the wise live their lives.[4]

1216. upadhīsu janā gadhitāse diṭṭhasute paṭighe ca mute ca
ettha vinodaya chandam anejo yo h'ettha na lippati taṃ munim āhu.

1216. Regarding objects of attachment, people are greedy for what is to be seen and heard and touched and otherwise experienced.[5] Being unmoved, dispel desire for them, for they call him a sage who does not cling to them.

1217. atha saṭṭhisitā savitakkā puthujjanatāya adhammaniviṭṭhā
na ca vaggagat'assa kuhiñci no pana duṭṭhullagāhī sa bhikkhu.

1217. Then, caught in the sixty,[6] full of (speculative) thoughts, because of being outsiders,[7] they are established in wrong teaching. But one who is a monk would not take up a sectarian viewpoint, much less seize upon what is bad.

1218. dabbo cirarattasamāhito akuhako nipako apihālu
santaṃ padam ajjhagamā muni paṭiccaparinibbuto kaṅkhati kālaṃ.

1218. Intelligent, for a long time composed (of mind), not deceitful, wise, not envious, the sage has experienced the peaceful state, depending on which, attained to quenching, he awaits his time.[8]

III. Despising the Well-behaved
(*Pesalā-atimaññanā*)

On another occasion, full of conceit because of his gift for composing extemporaneous verse, the Venerable Vangisa caught himself despising the other monks who were not so gifted. Repenting these thoughts, he composed the following poem:

1219. mānaṃ pajahassu Gotama mānapathañ ca jahassu asesaṃ
mānapathasmiṃ samucchito vippaṭisār'ahuvā cirarattaṃ.

1219. Abandon conceit, Gotama,[9] get rid of the way of conceit completely. Because of being infatuated by the way of conceit, for a long time you have been remorseful.

1220. makkhena makkhitā pajā mānahatā nirayaṃ <pa>patanti
socanti janā cirarattaṃ mānahatā nirayaṃ upapannā.

1220. Soiled by contempt (for others), destroyed by conceit, people fall into hell. Persons destroyed by conceit grieve for a long time upon being reborn in hell.

1221. na hi socati bhikkhu kadāci maggajino sammāpaṭipanno
kittiñ ca sukhañ c'anubhoti dhammadaso'ti tam āhu
tathattaṃ.

1221. A monk never grieves who is a knower of the path,[10] one who has practised it properly. He experiences fame and happiness; truthfully they call him "a seer of Dhamma."

1222. tasmā akhilo'dha padhānavā nīvaraṇāni pahāya visuddho
mānañ ca pahāya asesaṃ vijjāy'antakaro samitāvī.

1222. Therefore be without barrenness[11] here (in this world), energetic, purified by abandoning the hindrances. Having completely abandoned conceit, be an ender (of suffering) through knowledge and become one who dwells at peace.

IV. Ānanda

Once, soon after his ordination, Vangisa accompanied the Venerable Ananda on a visit to the house of one of the king's ministers. A number of women of the household came and paid reverence to the elder, asked questions, and listened to his preaching. But at the sight of these women sensual desire was aroused in Venerable Vangisa, which he immediately confessed to the Venerable Ananda. He recorded the incident in this poem:[12]

(Vaṅgīsa:)

1223. kāmarāgena ḍayhāmi cittaṃ me pariḍayhati
sādhu nibbāpanaṃ brūhi anukampāya Gotama.

1223. "I burn with sensual desire, my mind is enflamed (with passion). Out of pity please tell me, Gotama,[13] the effective extinguishing of it."

(Ānanda:)

1224. saññāya vipariyesā cittan te pariḍayhati
nimittaṃ parivajjehi subhaṃ rāgūpasaṃhitaṃ. (A)

1224. "Your mind is enflamed because of distorted perception. Shun the aspect of beauty associated with passion. (A)

1224. saṅkhāre parato passa dukkhato mā ca attato
nibbāpehi mahārāgaṃ mā ḍayhittha punappunaṃ. (B)

1224. "See constructions[14] as other, as painful, not as self, (and thus) extinguish strong passion; do not burn again and again. (B)[15]

1225. asubhāya cittaṃ bhāvehi ekaggaṃ susamāhitaṃ
sati kāyagatā ty atthu nibbidābahulo bhava.

1225. "Devote the mind, one-pointed and well-composed, to the contemplation of foulness.[16] Let mindfulness be directed towards the body and be full of disenchantment for it.

1226. animittañ ca bhāvehi mānānusayam ujjaha
tato mānābhisamayā upasanto carissasi.

1226. "Contemplate the signless[17] and cast out the underlying tendency to conceit. Then by the penetration of conceit you will go about at peace."

V. Well-spoken
(*Subhāsitā*)

These verses came to the Venerable Vangisa while he was listening to a talk delivered by the Buddha on the "well-spoken word." Having received permission from the Teacher, he then recited this poem in his presence:[18]

1227. tam eva vācaṃ bhāseyya yāy'attānaṃ na tāpaye
pare ca na vihiṃseyya sā ve vācā subhāsitā.

1227. One should speak only that word by which one would not torment oneself nor harm others. That word is indeed well spoken.

1228. piyavācam eva bhāseyya yā vācā paṭinanditā
yaṃ anādāya pāpāni paresaṃ bhāsate piyaṃ.

1228. One should speak only pleasant words, words which are acceptable (to others). What one speaks without bringing evils to others is pleasant.

1229. saccaṃ ve amatā vācā esa dhammo sanantano
sacce atthe ca dhamme ca āhu santo patiṭṭhitā.

1229. Truth is indeed the undying word; this is an ancient verity. Upon truth, the good say, the goal and the teaching are founded![19]

1230. yaṃ buddho bhāsatī vācaṃ khemaṃ nibbānapattiyā
dukkhass'antakiriyāya sa ve vācānam uttamā.

1230. The sure word the Awakened One speaks for the attainment of nibbāna, for making an end of suffering, is truly the best of words.

VI. Sāriputta

Verses spoken in praise of the Venerable Sariputta:

1231. gambhīrapañño medhāvī maggāmaggassa kovido
Sāriputto mahāpañño dhammaṃ deseti bhikkhunaṃ.

1231. Of profound wisdom, intelligent, skilled in knowledge of the right and wrong path, Sāriputta of great wisdom teaches Dhamma to the monks.

1232. saṃkhittena pi deseti vitthārena pi bhāsati
sālikāyeva nigghoso paṭibhānaṃ udiyyati.

1232. He teaches in brief, he speaks with detailed explanation, his voice is (pleasing) like that of the mynah bird; he demonstrates readiness of speech.[20]

1233. tassa taṃ desayantassa suṇantā madhuraṃ giraṃ
sarena rajanīyena savanīyena vaggunā
udaggacittā muditā sotaṃ odhenti bhikkhavo.

1233. Listening to his sweet utterance[21] while he is teaching with a voice that is captivating, pleasing, and lovely, the monks give ear, with minds elated and joyful.

VII. The Invitation Ceremony (*Pavāraṇā*)

Verses spoken in praise of the Buddha on an occasion of the Invitation Ceremony:[22]

1234. ajja pannarase visuddhiyā bhikkhū pañcasatā samāgatā
saṃyojanabandhanacchidā anīghā khīṇapunabbhavā isī.

1234. Today on the fifteenth (of the fortnight)[23] five hundred monks have gathered for the ceremony of purification, cutters of fetters and bonds, untroubled, seers finished with renewed existence.

1235. cakkavattī yathā rājā amaccaparivārito
samantā anupariyeti sāgarantam mahiṃ imaṃ
1236. evaṃ vijitasaṃgāmaṃ satthavāhaṃ anuttaraṃ
sāvakā payirupāsanti tevijjā maccuhāyino.

1235–36. As a wheel-turning monarch, surrounded by his ministers, tours all around this ocean-girt earth, so do the disciples with the threefold knowledge, who have left death behind, attend upon the victor in battle, the unsurpassed caravan leader.

1237. sabbe bhagavato puttā palāp'ettha na vijjati
taṇhāsallassa hantāraṃ vande ādiccabandhunaṃ.

1237. All are the Fortunate One's sons; there is no chaff found here. I pay homage to the destroyer of the dart of craving, the Kinsman of the Sun.

VIII. More than a Thousand (*Parosahassaṃ*)

A poem composed on the occasion of a Dhamma-talk concerning nibbana, delivered by the Buddha to a large company of monks:

1238. parosahassaṃ bhikkhūnaṃ sugataṃ payirupāsati
desentaṃ virajaṃ dhammaṃ nibbānaṃ akutobhayaṃ.

1238. More than a thousand monks attend upon the Happy One as he is teaching the stainless Dhamma concerning nibbāna, where no fear can come from any quarter.

1239. suṇanti dhammaṃ vimalaṃ sammāsambuddhadesitaṃ
sobhati vata sambuddho bhikkhusaṅghapurakkhato.

1239. They hear the taintless Dhamma taught by the Fully Awakened One. The Awakened One is truly resplendent as he is revered by the community of monks.

1240. nāganāmo'si bhagavā isīnaṃ isisattamo
mahāmegho va hutvāna sāvake abhivassasi.

1240. You are called a nāga,[24] Fortunate One; of seers, you are the best of seers.[25] Like a great rain-cloud, you rain down upon the disciples.

1241. divāvihārā nikkhamma satthudassanakamyatā
sāvako te mahāvīra pāde vandati Vaṅgiso.

1241. Leaving his daytime abode, wishing to see the Teacher, your disciple Vaṅgīsa pays homage at your feet, Great Hero.

IX. Overcoming
(*Abhibhuyya*)

Further verses composed by the Venerable Vangisa when the Buddha, after hearing the previous poem, invited him to speak more extemporaneous verses:[26]

1242. ummaggapathaṃ Mārassa abhibhuyya carati pabhijja khilāni
taṃ passatha bandhanamuñcaṃ asitaṃ va bhāgaso pavibhajja.

1242. Overcoming the devious ways and range of Māra, he walks (free), having broken up the things that make for barrenness of mind.[27] See him producing release from bonds, unattached, separating (the Teaching) into its constituent parts.[28]

1243. oghassa hi nittharaṇatthaṃ anekavihitaṃ <su->maggaṃ akkhāsi
tasmiñ ca amate akkhāte dhammadasā ṭhitā asaṃhīrā.

1243. He has shown the path in a variety of ways with the aim of guiding us across the flood. Since the undying has been shown (to them), the Dhamma-seers (are those who) stand immovable.

1244. pajjotakaro ativijjha sabbaṭṭhitīnam atikkamam addā
ñatvā ca sacchikatvā ca aggaṃ so desayi das'aḍḍhānaṃ.

1244. The light-maker, having penetrated (the Dhamma), saw the overcoming of all standpoints.[29] Having understood and experienced it, he taught the topmost (Dhamma-teaching) to the five.[30]

1245. evaṃ sudesite dhamme ko pamādo vijānataṃ dhammaṃ
tasmā <ti ha> tassa bhagavato sāsane appamatto sadā namassam anusikkhe.

1245. When the Dhamma has been thus well taught, what indolence could there be in those who know the Dhamma? Therefore, vigilant and ever revering, one should follow the training in the Fortunate One's dispensation.

X. Koṇḍañña

Verses composed on an occasion when the Elder Aññata Kondañña came to pay his respects to the Teacher:

1246. buddhānubuddho yo thero Koṇḍañño tibbanikkamo
lābhī sukhavihārānam vivekānaṃ abhiṇhaso.

1246. The Elder Koṇḍañña, strong in energy, who was enlightened after the Awakened One,[31] is repeatedly the obtainer of pleasurable abidings and seclusions.[32]

1247. yaṃ sāvakena pattabbaṃ satthusāsanakārinā
sabb'assa taṃ anuppattaṃ appamattassa sikkhato.

1247. Whatever is to be attained by a disciple who does the instruction of the Teacher, all that has been attained by him, vigilant and disciplined.

1248. mahānubhāvo tevijjo cetopariyakovido
Koṇḍañño buddhadāyādo pāde vandati satthuno.

1248. Having great power and the threefold knowledge, skilled in knowing the thoughts of others, Koṇḍañña, the Awakened One's heir, pays homage at the Teacher's feet.

XI. Moggallāna

Verses in praise of the Elder Mahamoggallana:

1249. nagassa passe āsīnaṃ muniṃ dukkhassa pāraguṃ
sāvakā pariyupāsanti tevijjā maccuhāyino.

1249. Disciples, possessors of the threefold knowledge who have left death behind, attend upon the sage seated on the mountain side, who has gone to the far shore beyond suffering.

1250. cetasā anupariyeti Moggallāno mahiddhiko
cittaṃ nesaṃ samanvesaṃ vippamuttaṃ nirūpadhiṃ.

1250. Moggallāna, of great supernormal powers, encompasses (their minds) with his mind, seeking their minds, completely freed, without attachments.[33]

1251. evaṃ sabbaṅgasampannaṃ muniṃ dukkhassa pāraguṃ
anekākārasampannaṃ payirupāsanti Gotamam.

1251. Thus do they attend upon Gotama endowed with so many virtuous qualities, the sage possessed of all the attributes and gone to the far shore beyond suffering.

XII. Gaggarā

Once when the Buddha was seated by the Gaggara Lotus-pond near the town of Campa, surrounded by a large assembly, the Venerable Vangisa composed this verse in his praise:

1252. cando yathā vigatavalāhake nabhe virocati vītamalo va bhānumā
evam pi Aṅgīrasa tvaṃ mahāmuni atirocasī yasasā sabbalokaṃ.

1252. As the moon shines in the sky free from clouds, as also the spotless sun, even so, Resplendent One, Great Sage, do you outshine the whole world with your fame.

XIII. Vaṅgīsa (1)

This, the Venerable Vangisa's "autobiographical" poem, was composed shortly after he attained arahantship:

1253. kāveyyamattā vicarimha pubbe gāmā gāmaṃ purā puraṃ
ath' addasāma sambuddhaṃ sabbadhammāna pāraguṃ.

1253. Intoxicated with skill in the poetic art, formerly we wandered from village to village, from town to town. Then we saw the Awakened One gone to the far shore beyond all (worldly conditioned) phenomena.

1254. so me dhammam adesesi muni dukkhassa pāragū
dhammaṃ sutvā pasīdimha saddhā no udapajjatha.

1254. The sage gone to the far shore beyond suffering taught me the Dhamma. On hearing the Dhamma we gained confidence in him; faith arose in us.

1255. tassāhaṃ vacanaṃ sutvā khandhe āyatanāni ca
dhātuyo ca viditvāna pabbajiṃ anagāriyaṃ.

1255. Having heard his word and learnt of the aggregates, bases, and elements, I went forth into homelessness.

1256. bahūnaṃ vata atthāya uppajjanti tathāgatā
itthīnaṃ purisānañ ca ye te sāsanakārakā.

1256. Indeed Tathāgatas appear for the good of the many men and women who practise their teaching.

1257. tesaṃ kho vata atthāya bodhiṃ ajjhagamā muni
bhikkhūnaṃ bhikkhunīnañ ca ye niyāmagataddasā.

1257. Indeed the sage attained enlightenment for the good of those monks and nuns who see the course to be undergone.[34]

1258. sudesitā cakkhumatā buddhenādiccabandhunā
cattāri ariyasaccāni anukampāya pāṇinaṃ.

1258. Well taught are the Four Noble Truths by the Seeing One, the Awakened One, the Kinsman of the Sun, out of compassion for living beings.

1259. dukkhaṃ dukkhasamuppādaṃ dukkhassa ca atikkamaṃ
ariyañ c'aṭṭhaṅgikaṃ maggaṃ dukkhūpasamagāminaṃ.

1259. Suffering, the origin of suffering, the overcoming of suffering, and the noble eightfold path leading to the allaying of suffering.

1260. evam ete tathā vuttā diṭṭhā me te yathātathā
sadattho me anuppatto kataṃ buddhassa sāsanaṃ.

1260. Thus these things, thus spoken of, have been seen by me as they really are. The true goal has been reached by me; the Awakened One's instruction has been done.

1261. svāgataṃ vata me āsi mama buddhassa santike
saṃvibhattesu dhammesu yaṃ seṭṭhaṃ tad upāgamiṃ.

1261. It was good indeed for me, my coming into the presence of the Awakened One. Among things shared out I obtained the best.

1262. abhiññāpāramippatto sotadhātuvisodhito
tevijjo iddhippatto'mhi cetopariyakovido.

1262. I have attained the perfection of the direct knowledges, I have purified the element of hearing, I have the threefold knowledge and obtained supernormal powers and am skilled in knowing the minds of others.

XIV. Vaṅgīsa (2)

The shorter version of the previous poem (at S I 196):

1. kāveyyamattā vicarimha pubbe gāmā gāmaṃ purā puraṃ
ath' addasāma sambuddhaṃ saddhā no udapajjatha.

1. Intoxicated with skill in the poetic art, formerly we wandered from village to village, from town to town. Then we saw the Awakened One and faith arose in us.

2. so me dhammam adesesi khandhe āyatanāni dhātuyo ca
tassāhaṃ dhammaṃ sutvāna pabbajiṃ anagāriyaṃ.

2. He taught me the Dhamma concerning the aggregates, bases, and elements. Having heard his Dhamma, I went forth into homelessness.

3. bahunnam vata atthāya bodhim ajjhagamā muni
bhikkhūnaṃ bhikkhunīnañ ca ye niyāmagataddasā.

3. Indeed the sage attained enlightenment for the good of the many monks and nuns who see the course to be undergone.

4. *svāgataṃ vata me āsi mama buddhassa santike*
tisso vijjā anuppattā kataṃ buddhassa sāsanaṃ.

4. It was good indeed for me, my coming into the presence of the Awakened One. The three knowledges have been attained; the Awakened One's instruction has been done.

5. *pubbenivāsaṃ jānāmi dibbacakkhuṃ visodhitaṃ*
tevijjo iddhippatto'mhi cetopariyāyakovido.

5. I know my former abodes, (I possess) the purified divine eye, I have the threefold knowledge and obtained supernormal powers and am skilled in knowing the minds of others.

XV. Nigrodhakappa

In this, the longest of the poems, the Venerable Vangisa asks the Buddha whether his deceased preceptor, the Elder Nigrodhakappa, had attained final nibbana. This provides an opportunity for Vangisa to sing the praises of the Buddha himself:

1263. *pucchāmi satthāram anomapaññaṃ*
diṭṭh'eva dhamme yo vicikicchānaṃ chettā
Aggāḷave kālam akāsi bhikkhu
ñāto yasassī abhinibbutatto.

1263. "I ask the teacher of superior wisdom, one who in this very life is the cutter-off of doubts: The monk, well known and famous, who has died at Aggāḷava, was he completely quenched in mind?

1264. *Nigrodhakappo iti tassa nāmaṃ*
tayā kataṃ bhagavā brāhmaṇassa
so taṃ namassam acari mutyapekho
āraddhaviriyo daḷhadhammadassī.

1264. "Nigrodhakappa was the name given to that brahmin by you, Fortunate One. Looking for release, strenuously energetic, he went about revering you, O seer of the secure state (i.e. nibbāna).

1265. taṃ sāvakaṃ Sakka mayam pi sabbe
aññātum icchāma samantacakkhu
samavaṭṭhitā no savanāya sotā
tuvaṃ nu satthā tvam anuttaro'si.

1265. "Sakka, All-seeing One, we all wish to know concerning that disciple. Our ears are ready to hear. You are the teacher, you are unsurpassed.

1266. chind'eva no vicikicchaṃ brūhi m'etaṃ
parinibbutaṃ vedaya bhūripañña
majjh'eva no bhāsa samantacakkhu
Sakko va devāna sahassanetto.

1266. "Sever our doubt. Tell me this, you of extensive wisdom, that he experienced quenching. Speak in our very midst, All-seeing One, like the thousand-eyed Sakka in the midst of the gods.

1267. ye keci ganthā idha mohamaggā
aññāṇapakkhā vicikicchaṭṭhānā
tathāgataṃ patvā na te bhavanti
cakkhuṃ hi etaṃ paramaṃ narānaṃ.

1267. "Whatever bonds exist here (in the world), ways of delusion, on the side of ignorance, bases for doubt, they no longer exist on reaching the Tathāgata, for that vision of his is supreme among men.

1268. no ce hi jātu puriso kilese
vāto yathā abbhaghanaṃ vihāne
tamo'v'assa nivuto sabbaloko
na jotimanto pi narā tapeyyuṃ.

1268. "If no man were ever to disperse the defilements as the wind disperses a mass of clouds, the whole world, enveloped, would surely be darkness, and even illustrious men would not shine forth.

1269. dhīrā ca pajjotakarā bhavanti
taṃ taṃ ahaṃ dhīra tath'eva maññe
vipassinaṃ jānam upāgamimha
parisāsu no āvikarohi Kappaṃ.

1269. "But the wise are light-makers. O Wise One, I think you are just such a one. We have come upon him who knows and is gifted with insight. Make evident to us, within the companies (of disciples), the fate of Kappa.

1270. khippaṃ giraṃ eraya vaggu vagguṃ
haṃso va paggayha sanikaṃ nikūja
bindussarena suvikappitena
sabb'eva te ujjugatā suṇoma.

1270. "Quickly enunciate your beautiful utterance, O beautiful one! Like a goose stretching forth (its neck), honk gently with your melodious and well-modulated voice; we are all listening to you attentively.

1271. pahīnajātimaraṇaṃ asesaṃ
niggayha dhonaṃ vadessāmi dhammaṃ
na kāmakāro hi puthujjanānaṃ
saṃkheyyakāro'va tathāgatānaṃ.

1271. "Pressing the one who has completely abandoned birth and death, I shall urge the purified one to speak Dhamma. For among outsiders there is no acting as they wish, but among Tathāgatas there is acting with discretion.[35]

1272. sampannaveyyākaraṇaṃ tavedaṃ
samujjupaññassa samuggahītaṃ
ayam añjali pacchimo suppaṇāmito
mā mohayi jānam anomapañña.

1272. "This full explanation of yours, (coming from) one with upright wisdom, is well learnt. This last salutation is proferred. You of superior wisdom, knowing (Kappa's fate), do not keep us in ignorance.

1273. parovaraṃ ariyadhammaṃ viditvā
mā mohayi jānam anomaviriya
vāriṃ yathā ghammanighammatatto
vācābhikaṅkhāmi sutaṃ pavassa.

1273. "Having known the noble Dhamma in its full extent, you of superior energy, knowing (Kappa's fate), do not keep us in ignorance. I long for your word as one overcome by heat in the hot season longs for water. Rain down on our ears.[36]

1274. yadatthiyaṃ brahmacariyaṃ acāri
Kappāyano kacci 'ssa taṃ amoghaṃ
nibbāyi so ādu saupādiseso
yathā vimutto ahu taṃ suṇoma.

1274. "Surely the purpose for which Kappāyana practised the holy life was not in vain. Was he quenched or had he a residue remaining?[37] Let us hear in what way he was released."

1275. acchecchi taṇhaṃ idha nāmarūpe
taṇhāya sotaṃ dīgharattānusayitaṃ
atāri jātimaraṇaṃ asesaṃ
icc abravī bhagavā pañcaseṭṭho.

1275. "He cut off craving here for mind-and-materiality", said the Fortunate One, "the stream of craving which for a long time had lain latent within him. He has crossed beyond birth and death completely." So spoke the Fortunate One, the foremost of the five.[38]

1276. esa sutvā pasīdāmi vaco te isisattama
amoghaṃ kira me puṭṭhaṃ na maṃ vañcesi brāhmaṇo.

1276. "On hearing your word, O best of seers, I believe. My question was truly not in vain; the brahmin did not deceive me.

1277. yathāvādī tathākārī ahū buddhassa sāvako
acchecchi Maccuno jālaṃ tataṃ māyāvino daḷhaṃ.

1277. "As he spoke, so he acted. He was a disciple of the Awakened One. He cut through the strong, spread-out net of Death the deceiver.

1278. addasa bhagavā ādiṃ upādānassa Kappiyo
accagā vata Kappāyano maccudheyyaṃ suduttaraṃ.

1278. "Kappiya saw the starting point of grasping, O Fortunate One. Kappāyana has certainly gone beyond the realm of Death, so difficult to cross.

1279. taṃ devadevaṃ vandāmi puttaṃ te dvipaduttama
anujātaṃ mahāvīraṃ nāgaṃ nāgassa orasaṃ.

1279. "I pay homage to you, the god of gods,[39] and to your son, O best of bipeds, to the great hero born in your tracks, a *nāga,* a true son of the *nāga.*"[40]

Appendices

I. Non-Canonical Verses of Vaṅgīsa

The Theragāthā, with the Vaṅgīsa-saṃyutta and the Suttanipāta, does not exhaust the verses ascribed to the Venerable Vaṅgīsa. Another pair of verses is attributed to him in the post-canonical *Milindapañha*, "The Questions of King Milinda" (p.390):

Yathā pi suriyo udayanto rūpaṃ dasseti pāṇinaṃ
suciñ ca asuciñ cāpi kalyāṇañ cāpi pāpakaṃ
tathā bhikkhu dhammadharo avijjāpihitaṃ janaṃ
pathaṃ dasseti vividhaṃ ādicco v'udayaṃ yathā ti.

Just as the sun rising in the sky shows shapes to creatures,
What is pure and what is impure, what is good and bad,
So the monk knowing Dhamma shows the path in various ways
To people cloaked in ignorance, as does the rising sun.

This work also contains verses ascribed to other elders, such as Sāriputta and Anuruddha, that are not to be found elsewhere. The *Milindapañha* records a dialogue between the Elder Nāgasena and King Milinda, the Indic form of the Greek name Menander. He is identified with a Greco-Bactrian king of the 2nd century B.C. who exercised rule in Northwest India. The work was probably composed originally in Prakrit or Sanskrit—even Greek has been suggested—and was subsequently translated into Pāli. It is therefore possible that these verses came from the Tipiṭaka of another Buddhist school, possibly the Sarvāstivāda.

There are also some verses extolling the virtues of the Buddha attributed to Vaṅgīsa (or Vāgīśa) in the Buddhist Hybrid Sanskrit work the *Mahāvastu*, which formed part of the Vinaya of the Lokuttaravādin school.[41] Among these is the following (p.130):

> As the glorious sun shines in the sky, and the full moon when the sky is clear, so dost thou, O Man, firm in concentration, shine forth like burnished gold.

This is reminiscent of Thag 1252. Then we find (p.131):

> Since through thine own understanding, thou has apprehended the truth and knowledge unheard of before, O Foremost Man, who shinest like thousand-eyed Maghavan,[42] pray give utterance to it.

This may be compared with Thag 1266. In the *Mahāvastu* itself the words, "pray give utterance to it," have no obvious connection with what has gone before or what follows, but they do have a significance in the Theragāthā context, where the poet questions the Buddha about the fate of Nigrodhakappa.

Another reference to Vaṅgīsa is found in the *Mahāvastu* when the Buddha addresses him thus, "Let there come to your mind, Vāgīśa, the recollection of a former association of yours with the Tathāgata." Vāgīśa then proceeds to tell in verse a story of a former life when the bodhisattva or Buddha-to-be, as a wise brahmin, was his teacher (pp.222f.).

II. Vaṅgīsa and the Vimānavatthu

The *Vimānavatthu* of the Khuddaka Nikāya is a collection of 83 stories in verse describing the *vimāna*—a kind of personal heavenly mansion—inhabited by beings reborn as gods or goddesses (*devatā*) as a reward for meritorious deeds performed by them as human beings. All the stories follow a similar pattern. They begin with an introductory verse (or verses) in which the god or goddess is asked about the cause for his or her rebirth with that particular mansion. The deva thereupon relates his or her previous good deeds.

Usually the Venerable Mahāmoggallāna is the questioner, but

occasionally another elder plays this role. Generally, it is only in the commentary that the questioner is named and the background supplied; otherwise the verses are anonymous. In four stories Vaṅgīsa is identified as the interlocutor: No. 16 (Sirimāvimāna), No. 35 (Sesavatīvimāna), No. 41 (Nāgavimāna), and No. 61 (another Nāgavimāna). In No. 37 (Visālakkhīvimāna) it is Sakka the ruler of the gods who questions the goddess. However, at the conclusion the commentary states that Sakka related it to Vaṅgīsa, who in turn told it to the compilers of the Canon.

We cannot be certain whether the ascription of these verses to Vaṅgīsa is authentic. There is nothing notable in the verses of the two Nāga mansion stories that can link them to the poet. If Vaṅgīsa did recite the verses of No. 37, although allegedly receiving them from Sakka, could they be regarded as his own composition? The introductory verses of Sesavatī are, interestingly enough, unique in the *Vimānavatthu* as constituting a seven-verse descriptive poem in its own right. There is none other comparable to it in length, and as it is ascribed to Vaṅgīsa, a translation of it is appended here. However, it is the Sirimā poem that is the most interesting of all the mansion stories, for it has a doctrinal content lacking elsewhere in the work. In it Sirimā describes how she became a disciple of the Buddha and a *sotāpanna*, one who has entered the stream leading to final emancipation. A translation of it is therefore presented as possibly a poetical work of Vaṅgīsa.

Sesavatī's Mansion

(Vaṅgīsa:)

"I see this delightful and beautiful mansion, its surface of many a colour, ablaze with crystal and roofed with silver and gold. A well-proportioned palace, possessing gateways, and strewn with golden sand.

As the thousand-rayed sun in the autumn shines in the sky in the ten directions, dispelling the dark, so does this your mansion glow, like a blazing smoke-crested fire in the darkness of the night.

It dazzles the eye like lightning, beautiful, suspended in space. Resounding with the music of lute, drum, and cymbals, this mansion of yours rivals Indra's city in glory.

White and red and blue lotuses, jasmine, and other flowers are there; blossoming sal trees and flowering asokas, and the air is filled with a variety of fragrances.

Sweet-scented trees, breadfruits, laden branches interlaced, with palm trees and hanging creepers in full bloom, glorious like jewelled nets; also a delightful lotus pool exists for you.

Whatever flowering plants there are that grow in water, and trees that are on land, those known in the human world and heavens, all exist in your abode.

Of what calming and self-restraint is this the result? By the fruit of what deed have you arisen here? How did this mansion come to be possessed by you? Tell it in full, O lady with thick eyelashes."

(Sesavatī:)

"How it come to be possessed by me, this mansion with its flocks of herons, peacocks, and partridges; and frequented by heavenly water-fowl and royal geese; resounding with the cries of birds, of ducks and cuckoos;

containing divers varieties of creepers, flowers and trees; with trumpet-flower, rose-apple, and asoka trees—now how this mansion came to be possessed by me, I will tell you. Listen, venerable sir.

In the eastern region of the excellent country of Magadha there is a village called Nālaka, venerable sir. There I lived formerly as a daughter-in-law and they knew me there as Sesavatī.

Scattering flower-blossoms joyfully I honoured him skilled in deeds and worshipped by gods and men, the great Upatissa[43] who has attained the immeasurable quenching.

Having worshipped him gone to the ultimate bourn, the eminent seer bearing his last body, on leaving my human shape I came to (the heaven of) the thirty (-three) and inhabit this place."

Vv. 642–53

Sirimā's Mansion

(Vaṅgīsa:)

"Your yoked and finely caparisoned horses, strong and swift, are heading downward through the sky. And these five hundred chariots, magically created, are following, the horses urged on by charioteers.

You stand in this excellent chariot, adorned, radiant and shining, like a blazing star. I ask you of lovely slender form and exquisite beauty, from which company of gods have you come to visit the Unrivalled One?"

(Sirimā)

"From those who have reached the heights of sensual pleasures, said to be unsurpassed; the gods who delight in magical transformation and creation. A nymph from that company able to assume any desired appearance has come here to worship the Unrivalled One."

(Vaṅgīsa:)

"What good conduct did you formerly practise here? How is it that you live in immeasurable glory and have gained such pleasures? Due to what have you acquired the unrivalled power to travel through the sky? Why does your beauty radiate in the ten directions?

You are surrounded and honoured by the gods. From where did you decease before you came to a heavenly bourn, goddess? Or of what teaching were you able to follow the word of instruction? Tell me if you were a disciple of the Awakened One."

(Sirimā)

"In a fine well-built city situated between hills, an attendant of a noble king endowed with good fortune, I was highly accomplished in dancing and singing. As Sirimā I was known in Rājagaha.

But then the Awakened One, the leader among seers, the guide, taught me of origination, of suffering and impermanence; of the unconditioned, of the cessation of suffering that is everlasting; and of this path, not crooked, straight, auspicious.

When I had learnt of the undying state (nibbāna), the unconditioned, through the instruction of the Tathāgata, the Unrivalled One, I was highly and well restrained in the precepts and established in the Dhamma taught by the most excellent of men, the Awakened One.

When I knew the undefiled place, the unconditioned, taught by the Tathāgata, the Unrivalled One, I then and there experienced the calm concentration (of the noble path). That supreme certainty of release was mine.

When I gained the distinctive undying, assured, eminent in penetrative insight, not doubting, I was revered by many people and experienced much pleasure and enjoyment.

Thus I am a goddess, knowing the undying, a disciple of the Tathāgata, the Unrivalled One; a knower of Dhamma established in the first fruit, a stream-enterer. Henceforth there is no bad bourn for me.

I came to revere the Unrivalled One and the virtuous monks who delight in what is skilled; to worship the auspicious assembly of ascetics and the respectworthy Fortunate One, the Dhamma-king.

I am joyful and gladdened on seeing the sage, the Tathāgata, the outstanding trainer of men capable of being trained, who has cut off craving, who delights in what is skilled, the guide. I worship the supremely merciful Compassionate One."

Vv. 137–49

Key to Abbreviations in Notes

A	Aṅguttara Nikāya
Ap	Apadāna
Be	Burmese-script edition of Thag (Sixth Council)
Comy.	Commentary
D	Dīgha Nikāya
Dhp	Dhammapada
Ee	European edition of Thag (PTS)
EV I	Elders' Verses I (K.R. Norman's trans. of Thag; PTS 1969)
It	Itivuttaka
M	Majjhima Nikāya
PTS	Pali Text Society
S	Saṃyutta Nikāya
Sn	Suttanipāta
SnA	Suttanipāta Commentary (Paramatthajotikā II)
Thag	Theragāthā
ThagA	Theragāthā Commentary (Paramatthadīpanī)
Ud	Udāna
Vism	Visuddhimagga
Vv	Vimānavatthu

(All references are to the PTS editions of Pāli texts unless indicated otherwise.)

Notes to the Pāli Text

References are by verse number and pāda

1211. (a) S: *ettato bhīyo*. (d) Reading *svamhi* = *so amhi* suggested by Norman.

1212. (a) Ee reads *sakiṃ*; Be and S read *sakkhī*; Norman suggests adverbial accusative *sakkhiṃ*.

1213. (a) I adopt the reading of S and other eds. of Thag. Ee has *evam evaṃ*. (d) Be and S read *pi dakkhasi* for *udikkhasi*.

1214. (d) I follow Norman's proposed amendation.

1215. (d) I read *mutattā* with Be and S, as against Ee *muttantā*.

1216. (d) I read with ThagA (text) and S: *taṃ munim āhu*.

1217. (a) I read *atha* with ThagA, Be, and S, as against Ee's *aṭṭha*. (c) I follow ThagA, Be, and S. (d) We should read, with S and other eds., *duṭṭhulla-* for Ee's *padulla-*.

1219. (c)–(d) I follow the reading proposed by Norman.

1220. (b) Norman suggests *papatanti* to regularize the cadence.

1222. (a) We should read *padhānavā* with ThagA, Be, and S, in place of Ee's *amānavā*.

1224B. This verse is not in Thag, but is included in S. ThagA also includes it in text, but without comment, which suggests it is not included in Thag's version of the poem.

1230. (a) S: *bhāsate*.

1232. (d) *udiyyati* follows Be, but ThagA (text and lemma) and S read *udīrayi*.

1237. (b) Reading *palāp'* with ThagA (text), Be, and S.

1239. (a) ThagA (text), Be, and S read *vimalaṃ* in place of Ee's *vipulaṃ* and that should be adopted.

1242. (c) The reading adopted is proposed by Norman in place of the established *bandhanapamuñcakaraṃ*.

1243. (b) The addition of *su* is proposed by Norman to normalize the metre.

1244. (d) I follow ThagA (text and lemma) in reading *das'aḍḍhānaṃ*. Although Ee and Be read *dasaddhānaṃ* (and S *dasatthānaṃ*), the gloss of ThagA (*pañcavaggiyānaṃ*) supports the reading adopted.

1245. (c) Norman suggests adding *ti ha* to normalize the metre.

1248. (c) S: *-pariyāya-*.

1249. (a) Ee's *nāgassa* is clearly an error and *nagassa* should be adopted.

1253. (c) The plural verb is consistent with *vicarimha* in (a) and is supported by ThagA (text and lemma), Be, and S.

1259. (c) Ee reads *ariyatthaṅgikaṃ*, but the reading I adopt is found in Be and tends to prevail in the tradition (see Dhp 191).

1265. (c) I read *sotā* with ThagA (text and lemma), Be, and Sn 345. A plural is needed to agree with *samavaṭṭhitā*. Norman suggests that *sotaṃ* may be an example of the change *-aṃ* < *-āni*.

1267. (a) *ganthā* should be adopted in place of Ee's *gandhā*.

1268. The reading of (d) follows Sn 348.

1269. (d) I follow ThagA (text and lemma), Be, and Sn 349 in reading *parisāsu* for Ee's *parisāya*.

1270. (b) Be with support of ThagA, and Sn 350, read *nikūja* in place of Ee's *nikūjaṃ*. Norman does not comment on the variant, but it seems this should be adopted.

1272. (b) ThagA (text and lemma), Be, and Sn 352 read *samujju-*, which should be adopted.

1273. (a) ThagA (text and lemma) and Be read *paroparaṃ*, but Sn 353 agrees with Ee in reading *parovaraṃ*.

Notes to the Translation

1. The Dark One (*kaṇha*) is another name for Māra the Evil One or Death (*maccu*, or *maccurāja*, the King of Death) in his aspect as *Kāmadeva*, the love god, the Indian Cupid. Like Cupid he also shoots arrows of passion at his victims. See Dhp 46: "plucking out the flower-tipped arrows of Māra, let him go beyond the sight of the King of Death." Hence also the last line of the poem: "You will not see my path."
2. The simile here is somewhat obscure. ThagA explains that whereas an archer can shoot only one arrow at a time, a woman assails all five senses simultaneously.
3. *Jagatogadhaṃ*, literally, "earth-plunged." ThagA whatever is mundane (*lokiya*), included in the three realms of being, conditioned.
4. Literally, "wander about."
5. *Muta* is a term for the other two senses, smell and taste, and can also refer to mind, the inner sense.
6. The cryptic expression "caught in the sixty" (*saṭṭhisitā*) seems to be an allusion to the sixty-two speculative views of the Brahmajāla Suttanta (D 1). Ven. Bhikkhu Bodhi points out (in a private communication) that the key to understanding this expression is found in the sutta itself, in the statement, *sabbe te imeh'eva dva-saṭṭhiyā vatthūhi antojālīkatā ettha sitā*.... "All these (ascetics and brahmins) are caught inside the net with its sixty-two divisions...." (D I 45).
7. On the term *puthujjana* see Introduction, pp.4–5.
8. The "peaceful state" is nibbāna, the extinguishing of the three "fires" of greed, hate, and delusion.
9. Vaṅgīsa here addresses himself as "Gotama," for as a disciple of the Buddha he regards himself as one of the Buddha's sons, a member of his spiritual family.
10. *Maggajina*. See Introduction, p.4.
11. *Akhila*, literally, "not barren." There are five things that hinder and prevent one from energetically pursuing the path, namely, doubt about the Teacher, the Dhamma, the Sangha, and the training, and resentment against one's companions in the holy life (M I 101). These things are called "mental barrennesses" (*cetokhila*); a mind obsessed

by them is likened to a piece of land that is of poor quality, with hard and stony soil, difficult to plough and producing no worthwhile crop.

12. At Vism I,103, the background to the verses is related differently. There it is said that lust arose in the Elder Vaṅgīsa when he saw an attractive woman while on alms round.
13. Here it is Ānanda, traditionally regarded as the Buddha's cousin, who is addressed as Gotama.
14. *Saṅkhāra*: all conditioned things comprised in the five aggregates.
15. See note to Pāli text.
16. The contemplation of the thirty-two parts of the body to overcome passion. Cf. Vism VIII, 42–144; M I 57, etc.
17. *Animittaṃ*. ThagA explains this as the distinguished contemplation of impermanence, because it pulls away the sign of permanence, etc.
18. The full sutta is at Sn pp.78–79 as well as at S I 188–89. Thag includes only Vaṅgisa's verses, but not the Buddha's verse.
19. ThagA assumes that *sacce* (truth), *atthe* (goal), and *dhamme* are all locatives. Here, however, I follow Norman's thesis that the verse was originally preserved in a Middle Indo-Aryan dialect in which the nominative singular ended in *-e* and was thus mistranslated into Pāli. I take *atthe* and *dhamme* as originally nominatives. For a fuller discussion, see EV I, p.292.
20. Or, spontaneity; *paṭibhāna* is also the word used to describe Vaṅgīsa's gift of unpremeditated poetic invention.
21. ThagA says this is an attribute of the voice of the mynah bird.
22. The *pavāraṇā* ceremony is held at the end of the rainy-season retreat (*vassa*). At this ceremony each monk invites the others to reproach him for any misdeed he might have committed during the retreat.
23. The night of the full moon.
24. See Introduction, p.5.
25. ThagA offers two explanations of *isisattamo*: the best seer (*uttamo isi*) among the seers such as disciples and paccekabuddhas; and the seventh seer (*sattamako isi*) counting from the Buddha Vipassī. Almost certainly the former explanation is correct, *sattama* being the superlative of *sat*. The second explanation alludes to the idea that Gotama is the seventh of the Buddhas often mentioned in the Canon (see D II 2–7).

26. This poem actually has no separate title as it is included with the previous poem in the Parosahassa Sutta of the Vaṅgīsa-saṃyutta. However, it is obviously a separate piece.
27. See note 11 above.
28. ThagA explains this to mean that the Buddha teaches by analysing the doctrine by way of its constituents such as the four foundations of mindfulness, etc.
29. ThagA explains the "standpoints" as either the standpoints for views (see M I 135–36) or the standpoints for consciousness (see D III 228, 253).
30. *Das'aḍḍhānaṃ*. Literally, "to the half-ten," i.e. five. ThagA says this refers to the group of five monks, headed by Koṇḍañña, to whom the First Sermon was addressed.
31. The first half of this verse is also to be found among Koṇḍañña's own verses (Thag 679). Koṇḍañña was the very first of the Buddha's followers to awaken to the Dhamma.
32. There are three kinds of seclusion (*viveka*): physical, mental, and complete freedom from defilements. The pleasurable abidings are the four meditative absorptions (*jhāna*).
33. Elsewhere Moggallāna, the chief disciple noted for his supernormal powers (*iddhi*), is shown as reading the minds of others. At Ud 5.5 he identifies an evil-minded person and ejects him from the assembly. Here he examines the minds of these monks to determine their level of attainment and discovers they are all arahants.
34. *Niyāma* = the noble path.
35. The second part of the verse is obscure. ThagA explains: "Among outsiders (*puthujjana*), trainees (*sekha*), and arahant disciples there is no ability to do whatever they wish; they cannot know or speak whatever they want. But the Tathāgatas act with discretion; their actions are preceded by wisdom. The point is that they can know or speak whatever they want."
36. I follow Norman's suggestion that *sutaṃ* here is a metrical adaptation for *sotaṃ*, ear. ThagA explains it as equivalent to *sadda*, the sound (of your voice). See EV I, pp.298–99.
37. Norman has misunderstood this verse (at EV I, p.116). The distinction the poet is making is not between the nibbāna element with residue (*saupādisesa*) and the nibbāna without residue (*anupādisesa*),

i.e. nibbāna during life and after death; for Nigrodhakappa is already dead. The question is: Did he die with a residue of defilements (as a non-returner) or without a residue of defilements (as an arahant). See the use of *saupādisesa* at M I 62–63.

38. The Buddha is regarded as the foremost, that is, the chief or leader and teacher of the group of five monks who heard the First Sermon. ThagA gives other explanations of the word, i.e. "controller of the five senses."
39. The highest amongst those classified as devas or "gods"—by birth (heavenly beings), convention (kings), and attainment (arahants).
40. On *nāga*, see Introduction, p.5. This final verse is not found in the Sn version and the entire poem is omitted from the Saṃyutta.
41. The *Mahāvastu*, trans. by J.J. Jones, Vol. I (PTS 1949). Page references are to this translation.
42. Another name for Sakka, the ruler of the gods.
43. The personal name of Sāriputta, who is said to have come originally from Nālaka.

THE BUDDHIST PUBLICATION SOCIETY